Catalogue of

Low-cost
Toilet Options

Social Marketing for Urban Sanitation

Water, Engineering and Development Centre,
Loughborough University,
Leicestershire, LE11 3TU, UK

ISBN: 978-1-84380-075-0

A catalogue record for this book is available from the British Library.

WEDC (The Water, Engineering and Development Centre) at Loughborough
University in the UK is one of the world's leading institutions concerned with
education, training, research and consultancy for the planning, provision and
management of physical infrastructure for development in low- and middleincome
countries.

This edition is reprinted and distributed by Practical Action Publishing.
Since 1974, Practical Action Publishing has published and disseminated books and
information in support of international development work throughout the world.
Practical Action Publishing trades only in support of its parent charity objectives
and any profits are covenanted back to Practical Action (Charity Reg. No. 247257,
Group VAT Registration No. 880 9924 76).

Introduction

This catalogue has been prepared to help house owners in low-income urban communities choose an appropriate low-cost toilet option. It is designed to be used by **toilet builders** or other NGO or government fieldworkers who support house owners in their decision. Specifically developed for use in Dar es Salaam, Tanzania, it can also be used in many other low-income urban communities.

The toilet options presented in the catalogue were developed on the basis of results from consumer research and tested in low-income urban communities. Toilet builders were trained in the construction of each design.

This catalogue is one of the outputs of the **Social Marketing for Urban Sanitation** research project funded by DFID. The research was conducted by WEDC, Loughborough University in partnership with the London School of Hygiene and Tropical Medicine; WaterAid, Dar es Salaam Urban Programme, Tanzania; and Trend Group, Kumasi, Ghana.

The catalogue contains the following toilet technologies and options:

1. **Pit toilet with water seal slab**
    - Slab with plastic pour flush pan
    - Slab with ceramic pour flush pan

2. **Pit toilet without water seal**
    - Sanplat slab
    - Dome slab

3. **Compost toilets (Ecosan)**
    - Urine diversion slab

The catalogue shows three segments of a toilet: (i) the pit (lined/unlined),
(ii) the slab or platform and
(iii) the superstructure.

Guidelines for using the catalogue

The catalogue is organised to assist house owners to make the right choice of toilet technology.

- The top section of each page shows various types of superstructure ranging from temporary measures to more permanent types.
- The middle section of each page shows slabs or platforms (non-water seal and water seal) and water seal slabs connected to pits.
- The bottom section of each page shows pits (unlined and lined single & double, raised pit).

Pit toilets (Pour Flush; Dome; Sanplat)

When discussing toilets with individual house owners or groups, inform them about the various technologies in this catalogue. Show them pictures of the technologies and the various options available for them to choose from. Assist them to make a choice based on their individual circumstances and available resources. Where the individual involved is a man, always try to persuade them to involve women in the discussion and decision.

- The life span of a toilet depends on the size of the pit and the number of users.
- Where there are many users, it may be advisable to have alternating pits.
- Where the soil is unstable, it is always advisable to line the pits with blocks (trapezoidal blocks – a cheaper option), cement rings, or stones.

Pits

Begin by explaining about the pit and show them the various options of pits - unlined single/double; lined single/double and raised pits. Explain the approximate cost of the pit excavation and the cost of different types of lining (trapeziodal blocks, sand cement ring, and normal blocks). Remember that toilets in unstable soil must be lined and those in areas of high water table raised. The recommended pit dimensions are as follows:

- Depth of pit (in low water table): usually **2.8 - 3.0m**
- Depth of pit (in high water table): usually **1 - 1.5m**
- Where there is high water table, the pit should be raised above ground by about **0.5m**
- Breadth/Width of pit: usually **1.5m**

Remember to discuss the issue of emptying the pits when they are full. Direct pit toilets are often more difficult to empty that offset double pits, which have easier access.

Slabs

Explain the cost of the various slabs and the advantages and disadvantages of each. Assist the house owner in choosing the slab that will fit his situation. If they have an existing toilet, explore to see if it can be improved by adding one of the slabs. This may be a cheaper option than starting a new toilet.

Superstructure

Show them the various superstructures and explain the cost implications. Start with the cheapest, and explain to them that it could be a temporary measure until they are able to put in a more permanent structure.

Ecosan toilet

Following the discussion on pit toilets, go on to explain the Ecosan technology to them. Explain the various segments of the Ecosan toilet and the advantages and disadvantages. Discuss the maintenance process for the Ecosan toilet, which is very important for ensuring that it functions properly.

Vault

Show them the drawing of the Ecosan vault; explain that is advisable to have two vaults so that when one fills up, they can transfer to the second.

Slabs

The next thing is to show them the drawing of the single urine diversion slab, explaining how it works and the reason for separating the urine. Then go ahead and show them the drawing of the integrated double slabs and also explain why there needs to be double slab.

Superstructure

The discussion should follow the same process as that of the pit toilet. Also discuss the procedure for emptying a full Ecosan chamber and show them the drawing.

Note

They should wait for 1.5 – 2 years before a full Ecosan chamber is emptied and the sludge can be used as fertiliser.

At the time of compiling this catalogue the exchange rate for Tanzania Shillings (Tsh):
Tsh 1105 = $1 (USD)
Tsh 2000 = £1 (British Pound)

The costs shown includes labour charges and most of the expenses for completing each of the components. The cost is likely to change depending on the market price of materials.

Superstructure made with Nylon Rice Sacks

Cost estimate: = Tsh 12,000

Advantages

- Cheap
- Quick to install and can be roofed with any material
- Can be upgraded to timber or roofing sheet structure

Disadvantages

- Easily damaged by severe weather or people
- Sack may require replacement at short intervals

Single Sanplat (Sungura)

Cost estimate: = Tsh 2,700 (60cm x 60cm)

Advantages

- Low cost
- Easy to clean and maintain
- Long lasting and can be moved to another pit
- Easy to transport and install

Disadvantages

- Often too small to install on its own, requires wooden platform
- May be slippery especially where toilet is also used for bathing
- They can produce smell when the lid is lifted and users may not like this as the smell attracts flies

Unlined Single Pit

Cost estimate: Tsh 10,000

Advantages

- Can be very cheap to build
- Lasts for a long time in stable soil
- Pit is stronger when it is narrower at the base and wider at the top

Disadvantages

- Pits will collapse in unstable soil
- Not advisable in soft/sandy soil
- May be difficult to empty pit

Superstructure made with Wood

Cost estimate: = Tsh 26,000 (without roofing sheets) and Tsh 61,000 (with roofing sheets)

Advantages

- Relatively low-cost
- More permanent structure and can be roofed with any other material
- Stronger and less easy to damage
- Old wood can be used

Disadvantages

- May be expensive where used wooden planks are not easily available

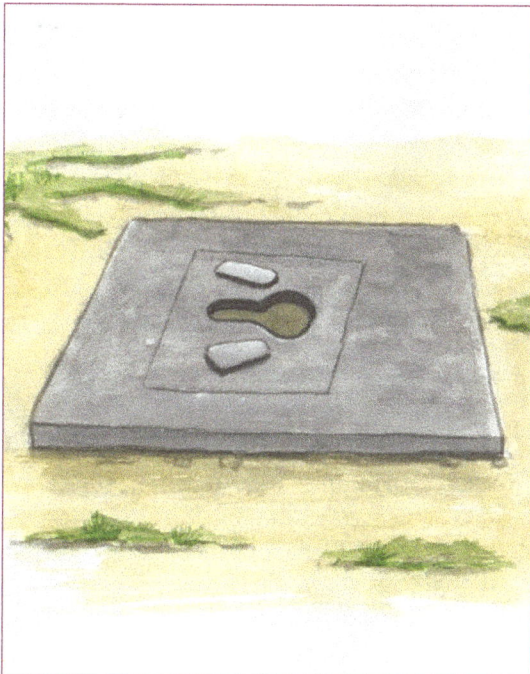

Integrated Sanplat (Sungura)

Cost estimate: = Tsh 22,000 (150cm x 150cm)

Advantages

- Easy to clean and maintain
- Long lasting
- Can be installed on its own without wooden platform

Disadvantages

- High cost
- Requires skilled labour for fabrication
- May be slippery especially where toilet is also used for bathing
- Very heavy to transport and better made near the toilet

Pit lined with Sand-Cement Rings
(6 rings = 1.5m x 2.8m pit)

Cost estimate: Pit excavation (Tsh 10,000) + Lining (Tsh 29,000) = Tsh 39,000

Advantages

- It is permanent and prevents soil from collapsing
- Safer option for lining in soft and sandy soil
- Possible to empty full pit and reuse it many times

Disadvantages

- Relatively expensive
- Rings can break during transportation and installation
- Emptying could be costly and there may be a problem with space to dispose of the sludge
- If the sludge is left for 1.5 - 2 years until it is safe to handle, users will have to look for an alternative toilet

Corrugated Iron Sheet Superstructure

Cost estimate: = Tsh 31,500 (without roofing sheets) and Tsh 66,500 (with roofing sheets)

Advantages

- Stronger and less easy to damage
- More permanent structure
- Old corrugated iron sheets can be used to make it cheaper
- Not damaged easily by rain or sun

Disadvantages

- Relatively expensive
- Rusts easily and may need replacement
- Could get quite hot during the day

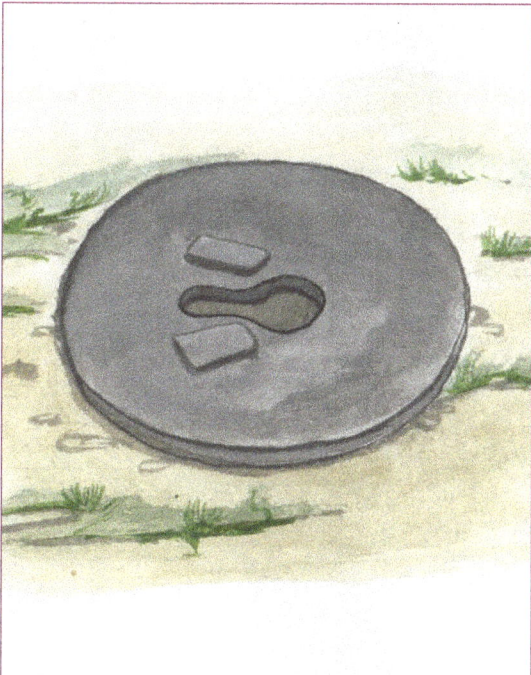

Dome Slab

Cost estimate: = Tsh 7,100 (1.2m) with concrete cover = Tsh 10,150 (1.5m)

Advantages

- Low cost
- Easy to clean and maintain
- Long lasting and can be moved to another pit
- Easy to install

Disadvantages

- May be slippery especially where toilet is also used for bathing
- They can produce smell when the lid is lifted and users may not like this as the smell attracts flies
- Could be heavy to transport, especially the 1.5m slab

Pit lined with Trapezoidal Cement Blocks

Cost estimate: Pit excavation (Tsh 10,000) + Lining (Tsh 38,000) = Tsh 48,500

Advantages

- It is permanent and prevents soil from collapsing
- Pit can be emptied and reused many times
- Blocks are less likely to break during transportation and installation

Disadvantages

- High cost
- Requires special mould for fabricating blocks and skilled labour for lining.
- Emptying could be costly and there may be a problem with space to dispose of the sludge
- If the sludge is left for 1.5 - 2 years until it is safe to handle, users will have to look for an alternative toilet

Cement Block Superstructure (1.2m x 1.2m) without Vent Pipe

Cost estimate: = Tsh 56,000 (without roofing sheets) and Tsh 91,000 (when roofed with iron sheets)

Advantages
- Lasts for a very long time
- Permanent structure
- Can reduce smell and heat

Disadvantages
- Expensive

Direct Pit Dome Slab with Pour Flush Pan (plastic and ceramic)

Cost estimate:

1.2m dome + plastic pour flush pan = Tsh 10,500

1.5m dome + plastic pour flush pan = Tsh 13,600

1.2m dome + ceramic pour flush pan = Tsh 15,500

1.5m dome + ceramic pour flush pan = Tsh 18,550

Advantages
- Easy to clean and maintain
- Controls smell and prevents flies entering the pit
- Fairly cheap and long lasting
- Allows for water to be used for anal cleansing

Disadvantages
- Requires water for use and maintenance
- May be slippery especially where toilet is also used for bathing

Raised Pit lined with Sand-Cement Rings
(3 rings = 1.0m below & 0.5m above ground)

Cost estimate: (Tsh 3,300) + Lining (Tsh 14,400) = Tsh 17,700

Advantages
- It is permanent and prevents soil from collapsing
- Safer option for lining in soft/sandy soil and in areas with high water table.
- Possible to empty full pit and reuse it many times

Disadvantages
- Relatively high cost
- Rings can break during transportation and installation
- Emptying could be costly and there may be a problem with space to dispose of the sludge.
- Pit could fill up quickly and if the sludge is left for 1.5 - 2 years until it is safe to handle, users will have to look for an alternative toilet

Cement Block Superstructure (1.2m x 1.2m) with Vent Pipe

Cost estimate: = Tsh 56,000 (without roofing sheets) and Tsh 91,000 (with roofing sheets)

Advantages
- Lasts for a very long time
- Permanent structure
- Can reduce smell and heat

Disadvantages
- Expensive

Dome Slab with Pour Flush Pan for Single Offset Toilet (plastic and ceramic)

Cost estimate:
1.2m dome + plastic pour flush pan = Tsh 11,300
1.5m dome + plastic pour flush pan = Tsh 21,600
1.2m dome + ceramic pour flush pan = Tsh 23,500
1.5m dome + ceramic pour flush pan = Tsh 26,550

Advantages
- Easy to clean and maintain
- Controls smell and prevents flies entering the pit
- Sludge can be flushed to external pit

Disadvantages
- Requires large quantity of water for use and maintenance
- Pipe can be blocked if not used properly
- May be slippery especially where toilet is also used for bathing

Raised Pit lined with Trapezoidal Cement Blocks

Cost estimate: Tsh 10,000 + Lining (Tsh 20,600) = Tsh 30,600

Advantages
- It is permanent and prevents soil from collapsing
- Suitable for lining in areas with high water table
- Pit can be emptied and reused many times
- Blocks are less likely to break during transportation and installation

Disadvantages
- High cost
- Requires special mould for fabricating blocks and skilled labour for lining
- Emptying could be costly and there may be a problem with space to dispose of the sludge.
- If the sludge is left for 1.5 - 2 years until it is safe to handle, users will have to look for an alternative toilet

Cement Block Superstructure (1.2m x 1.2m) with Vent Pipe on a Raised Pit

Cost estimate: = Tsh 56,000 (without roofing sheets) and Tsh 85,000 (with roofing sheets)

Advantages
- Lasts for a very long time
- Permanent structure
- Can reduce smell and heat

Disadvantages
- Expensive

Offset Pour Flush Slab & Single Pit lined with Sand-Cement Rings (plastic and ceramic)

Cost estimate:

Dome + plastic pan + sand-cement ring lined pit & cover = (1.2m: Tsh 57,400); (1.5m: Tsh 67,700)

Dome + ceramic pan + sand-cement ring lined pit & cover = (1.2m: Tsh 69,600); (1.5m: Tsh 72,650)

Advantages
- Easy to clean and maintain
- Controls smell and prevents flies entering the pit
- Sludge can be flushed to external pit
- Easy access for emptying full pit

Disadvantages
- Relatively high cost
- Needs large quantity of water for use and maintenance
- Pipe can be blocked if not used properly
- May be expensive to empty full pit

Unlined Double Pit

Cost estimate: Tsh 20,000

Advantages
- Low cost
- Lasts longer that single pit in stable soil
- Possible to move from one pit to the other when one is full
- Sludge from the full pit can be used as fertiliser after 1.5 – 2 years

Disadvantages
- Pits will collapse in unstable soil
- Not advisable in soft/sandy soil
- It may not be possible to use sludge for fertiliser where agriculture is not practised
- May be difficult to empty pit

Cement Block Superstructure (1.2m x 1.2m) with Vent Pipe on a Raised Pit

Cost estimate: = Tsh 56,000 (without roofing sheets) and Tsh 85,000 (with roofing sheets)

Advantages
- Lasts for a very long time
- Permanent structure
- Can reduce smell and heat

Disadvantages
- Expensive

Offset Pour Flush Slab & Single Pit lined with Sand-Cement Rings (plastic and ceramic)

Cost estimate:
Dome + plastic pan + sand-cement ring lined pit & cover = (1.2m: Tsh 57,400); (1.5m: Tsh 67,700)
Dome + ceramic pan + sand-cement ring lined pit & cover = (1.2m: Tsh 69,600); (1.5m: Tsh 72,650)

Advantages
- Easy to clean and maintain
- Controls smell and prevents flies entering the pit
- Sludge can be flushed to external pit
- Easy access for emptying full pit

Disadvantages
- Relatively high cost
- Needs large quantity of water for use and maintenance
- Pipe can be blocked if not used properly
- May be expensive to empty full pit

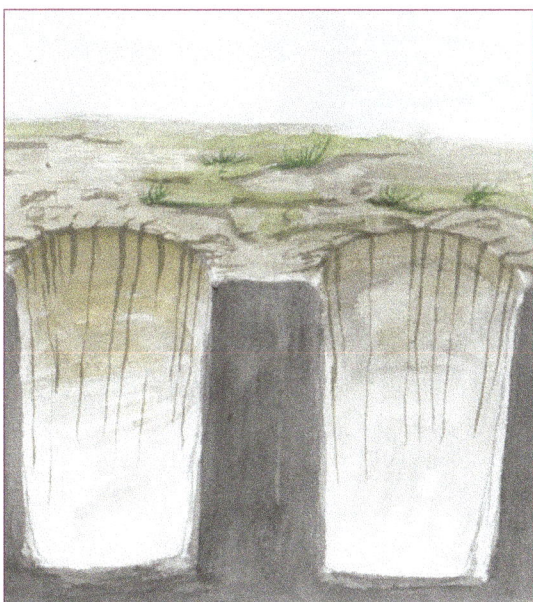

Unlined Double Pit

Cost estimate: Tsh 20,000

Advantages
- Low cost
- Lasts longer that single pit in stable soil
- Possible to move from one pit to the other when one is full
- Sludge from the full pit can be used as fertiliser after 1.5 – 2 years

Disadvantages
- Pits will collapse in unstable soil
- Not advisable in soft/sandy soil
- It may not be possible to use sludge for fertiliser where agriculture is not practised
- May be difficult to empty pit

Plastered Cement Block Superstructure without Vent Pipe

Cost estimate: = Tsh 68,700 (without roofing sheets) and Tsh 97,000 (with roofing sheets)

Advantages

- Lasts for a very long time
- Permanent structure
- Easy to paint with any colour

Disadvantages

- Very expensive

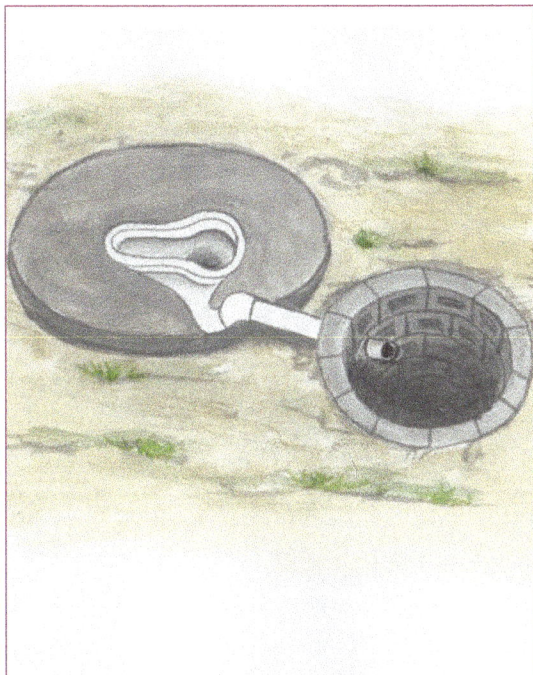

Offset Pour Flush Slab & Single Pit lined with Trapezoidal Blocks (plastic and ceramic)

Cost estimate:
Dome + plastic pan + trapezoidal block lined single pit & cover = (1.2m: Tsh 66,900); (1.5m: Tsh 77,200)
Dome + ceramic pan + trapezoidal block lined single pit & cover = (1.2m: Tsh 79,100); (1.5m: Tsh 82,150)

Advantages

- Easy to clean and maintain
- Controls smell and prevents flies entering the pit
- Sludge can be flushed to external pit
- Easy access for emptying full pit

Disadvantages

- High cost
- Needs large quantity of water for use and maintenance
- Pipe can be blocked if not used properly
- May be expensive to empty full pit

Double Pit lined with Sand-Cement Rings
(6 rings = 1.5m x 2.8m pit)

Cost estimate: Pit excavation (Tsh 20,000) + Lining (Tsh 58,000) = Tsh 78, 000

Advantages

- It is more permanent and could last for a very long time
- It prevents soil from collapsing
- The second pit can be used when the first pit is full and users do not have to look for an alternative toilet
- Sludge from the first pit can be safely removed and used as fertiliser after 1.5 – 2 years

Disadvantages

- Can be quite expensive
- Rings can break during transportation and installation
- People may not be interested in using sludge as fertiliser especially where farming is not practised

Plastered Cement Block Superstructure with Vent Pipe

Cost estimate: = Tsh 68,700 and Tsh 103,400 (with roofing sheets)

Advantages
- Lasts for a very long time
- Permanent structure
- Easy to paint with any colour
- Can reduce smell and heat

Disadvantages
- Very expensive

Dome Slab with Pour Flush Pan for Double Pit Offset Toilet (plastic and ceramic)

Cost estimate:
Dome + plastic pour flush pan = (1.2m: Tsh 13,300);
(1.5m: Tsh 23,600)
Dome + ceramic pour flush pan =(1.2m: Tsh 25,500);
(1.5m: Tsh 28,550)

Advantages
- Easy to clean and maintain
- Controls smell and prevents flies entering the pit
- Sludge can be flushed to external pit
- Enables the use of a second pit when the first one is full

Disadvantages
- High cost
- Needs large quantity of water for use and maintenance
- Pipe can be blocked if not used properly
- May be slippery when toilet is also used for bathing

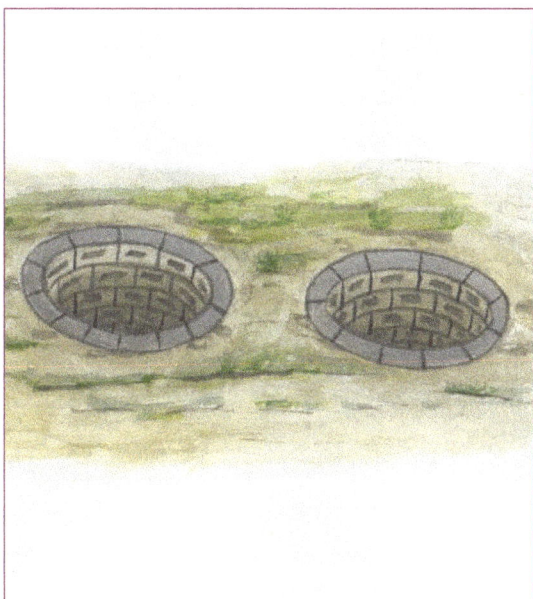

Double Pit lined with Trapezoidal Cement Blocks

Cost estimate: Pit excavation (Tsh 20,000) + Lining
(Tsh 77,000) = Tsh 97,000

Advantages
- It is more permanent and prevents soil from collapsing
- Pit can be emptied and reused many times
- Sludge from the first pit can be safely removed and used as fertiliser after 1.5 – 2 years
- Blocks are less likely to break during transportation and installation

Disadvantages
- Very high cost
- Requires special mould for fabricating blocks and skilled labour for lining
- People may not be interested in using sludge as fertiliser especially where farming is not practised

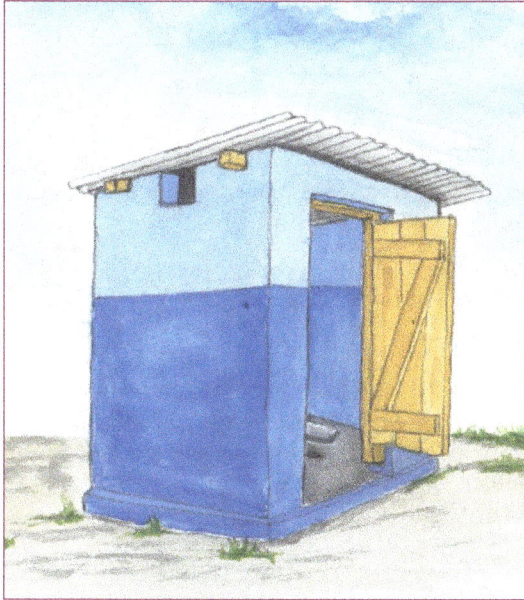

Painted Cement Block Superstructure without Vent Pipe

Cost estimate: = Tsh 72,700 (without roofing sheets) and Tsh 101,400 (with roofing sheets)

Advantages

- Lasts for a very long time
- Permanent structure
- Attractive

Disadvantages

- Highly expensive

Offset Pour Flush Slab & Double Pit lined with Sand-Cement Rings (plastic and ceramic)

Cost estimate:

Dome + plastic pan + sand-cement rings lined double pit & cover = (1.2m: Tsh 98,400); (1.5m: Tsh 108,700)

Dome + ceramic pan + sand-cement rings lined double pit & cover = (1.2m: Tsh 122,500); (1.5m: Tsh 125,550)

Advantages

- Pit can be emptied and reused many times
- Easy access for emptying full pit
- Easy to move to a second pit when the first pit is full and sludge can be used as fertiliser after 1.5 –2 years
- Suitable for houses with multiple families

Disadvantages

- High cost
- Rings may break during transportation and or installation
- May be expensive to empty full pit especially where people are not interested in using sludge for fertiliser

Raised Double Pit lined with Concrete Rings

Cost estimate: (Tsh 20,000) + Lining (Tsh 28,000) = Tsh 48,000

Advantages

- It can prevent flooding of toilets
- The second pit can be used when the first pit is full and users do not have to look for an alternative toilet
- Sludge from the first pit can be safely removed and used as fertiliser after 1.5 – 2 years

Disadvantages

- Can be quite expensive
- Rings can break during transportation and installation
- People may not be interested in using sludge as fertiliser especially where farming is not practised

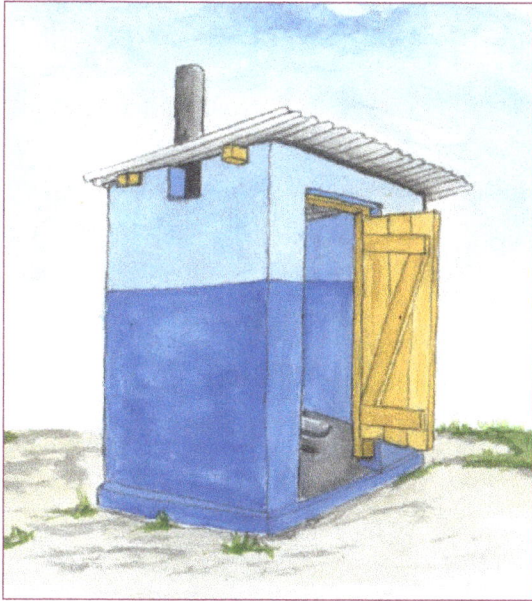

Painted Cement Block Superstructure with Vent Pipe

Cost estimate: = Tsh 72,700 and Tsh 101,400 (with roofing sheets)

Advantages
- Lasts for a very long time
- Permanent structure
- Attractive
- Can reduce smell and heat

Disadvantages
- Highly expensive

Offset Pour Flush Slab & Double Pit lined with Trapezoidal Blocks (plastic and ceramic)

Cost estimate:
Dome + plastic pan + trapezoidal block lined double pit & cover = (1.2m: Tsh 117,400); (1.5m Tsh 127,700)
Dome + ceramic pan + trapezoidal block lined double pit & cover = (1.2m: Tsh 129,600); (1.5m: Tsh 132,650)

Advantages
- Permanent structure
- Pit can be emptied and reused many times
- Sludge can be flushed to external pit
- Easy access for emptying full pit
- Easy to move to a second pit when the first pit is full and sludge can be used as fertiliser after 1.5 –2 years

Disadvantages
- High cost
- Requires skilled labour for making and lining with trapezoidal blocks
- May be expensive to empty full pit especially where people are not interested in using sludge for fertiliser

Raised Double Pit lined with Trapezoidal Cement Blocks

Cost estimate: (Tsh 20,000) + Lining (Tsh 20,600) = Tsh 40,600

Advantages
- It is more permanent and could last for a very long time
- Suitable for areas with high water table
- It can prevent flooding of toilets
- The second pit can be used when the first pit is full and users do not have to look for an alternative toilet
- Sludge can be safely removed and used as fertiliser after 1.5 – 2 years

Disadvantages
- Very high cost
- Requires special mould for fabricating blocks and skilled labour for lining

Plastered Cement Superstructure for Ecosan Toilet - 200cm x 115cm (emptying)

Cost estimate: = Tsh 150,000

Advantages

- Compost is usually dry and can be used as fertiliser or disposed of
- Compost can be sold to garden centres or vegetable growers especially in urban areas
- Urine can easily be removed and used as fertiliser
- Provides easy access for the removal of sludge to be used as fertiliser after 1.5 –2 years

Disadvantages

- High cost
- Requires skilled labour
- May not be suitable in areas where people are reluctant to handle this type of compost
- Risk of removing sludge before it becomes harmless especially in houses with many families

Double Compartment Ecosan Substructure

Cost estimate:
Single slab (60cm x 60cm)= Tsh 2,700
Double slab integrated (200cm x 115cm) = Tsh 83,850

Advantages

- Permanent structure
- Does not require pit
- Diverts urine away from faeces thereby reducing smell
- Urine can easily be removed and used as fertiliser
- Provides easy access for the removal of compost to be used as fertiliser after 1.5 –2 years

Disadvantages

- Relatively expensive and requires fair amount of space
- Requires skilled labour
- May not be suitable for houses with many families
- Requires special care and maintenance by users
- Can produce smell if not used and maintained properly when water is used for anal cleansing or toilet is used for bathing

Double Compartment Vault for Ecosan Toilet

Cost estimate: = Tsh 51, 900 (200cm x 115cm)

Advantages

- Permanent structure
- Easy to construct and does not require pit
- Provides easy access for the removal of sludge to be used as fertiliser after 1.5 –2 years

Disadvantages

- Relatively expensive
- Requires fair amount of space
- May not be suitable for houses with many families

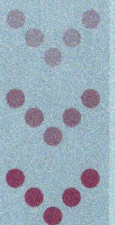

Toilet Construction Materials

This document is an output from a project funded by the UK. Department for International Development (DFID) for the benefit of low-income countries. The views expressed are not necessarily those of DFID.

Produced in partnership with:

London School of Hygiene and Tropical Medicine (LSHTM)
Keppel Street, London WC1E 7HT

Training, Research and Networking for Development (TREND)
P.O.Box 6808, Kumasi, Ghana

WaterAid
Prince Consort House, 27-29 Albert Embankment, London, SE1 7UB, UK.

Water, Engineering and Development Centre (WEDC)
Loughborough University, Leicestershire LE11 3TU UK